TREAT HER LIKE A
Lady

Treat Her Like A

Robert J. Poole, Jr.

Hunter Heart Publishing
DuPont, Washington

Hunter Heart Publishing
P.O. Box 354
DuPont, Washington 98327
www.hunterheartpublishing.com

Treat Her Like A Lady
Copyright © 2010 Robert J. Poole, Jr.
All Rights Reserved.

First Printing: September 2010

Unless otherwise indicated, all scripture is taken from the New King James Version of the Bible. "Scripture taken from the New King James Version. Copyright © 1982 by Thomas Nelson, Inc. Used by permission. All rights reserved."

"Scripture taken from *The Message*. Copyright © 1993, 1994, 1995, 1996, 2000, 2001, 2002. Used by permission of NavPress Publishing Group."

Scripture quotations marked NLT are taken from the Holy Bible, New Living Translation, copyright 1996, 2004. Used by permission of Tyndale House Publishers, Inc., Wheaton, Illinois 60189. All rights reserved.

Cover designer: Exousia Marketing Group, LLC
www.exousiamg.com

Printed in the United States of America.

ISBN: 978-0-9828377-1-9

This book or parts thereof may not be reproduced in any form, stored in a retrieval system, or transmitted in any form by any means- electronic, mechanical, photocopy, recording or otherwise- without prior permission of the publisher, except as provided by United States of America copyright law.

Dedication

This book is dedicated to my wife; the sugar in my coffee, the honey in my tea, the straw in my berry; God's beloved gift to me. Sheila you are the complete compliment to the fulfillment of my destiny. I love you!

Acknowledgments

I would like to thank Joshua and Shekinah, my pride and joy, for being such wonderful children. Daddy loves you! I also would like to thank Tressa Fernandez for your editing inputs. I thank you Destiny Christian Center for allowing me to be your lead sheep.

A sincere and heart felt thanks to Deborah Hunter and Hunter Heart Publishing. I am truly grateful for your labor of love, excellence, and professionalism on my book. God bless you!

Finally, I would like to thank the four men who helped make me who I am.

The Bible says in 1 Corinthians 4:15 "For though you might have ten thousand instructors in Christ, yet [you do] not [have] many fathers; for in Christ Jesus I have begotten you through the gospel."

Thank you Pop: Rev. Robert J. Poole, Sr., for teaching me how to love God's church. Thank you, Bishop A. J. Thompson, for teaching me to fall in love with God's Word. Thank you, Apostle Lee Rice, for being an ensample and example to me on how to love God's gift to me. Thank you, Bishop Nate Holcomb, for displaying daily before me that it's all about God's Son; it truly is all about Him!

Foreword

In his book, **<u>Treat Her Like A Lady</u>**, Pastor Robert Poole has tapped into the heart of God for understanding covenant relationships in marriage. Pastor Poole immediately grasps our attention in his book with the following statement:

> *"The institution of marriage today is under severe attack. The divorce rate is deceiving because, even though divorce is on the decline, more and more couples are living together without "the papers".*

Pastor Poole's response to this assault on marriages is God's response. *"Husbands, love your wives, even as Christ also loved the church, and gave himself for it* (Ephesians 5:25). Pastor Poole then states that according to Ephesians 5:25, agape is known as *"the love of choice."* The love of choice or the love with which Christ loves us is agape. Agape always puts the one it loves before itself. Agape is the God-kind of love.

It is with wit, humor, and the sincerity of the heart of God that Pastor Poole charts a course for us that unwraps the practical, pragmatic components of loving our wives as Christ loves the church.

In this book, with uncompromising resolve, Pastor Poole displays the fact that it is agape that shows to us *"the light, the life and love of Jesus Christ"* in marriage. With Jesus as the center and circumference, the base and the boundary, the beauty and the balance, the sum and the substance of our marriages, we are taught and trained to operate and walk in the love of choice; which is agape.

It is my prayer that through this book you will receive additional insight for oversight that imparts the heart of the Father for our marriages; as the Father Himself declares in Genesis 2:24 KJV: *"Therefore shall a man leave his father and his mother, and shall cleave unto his wife: and they shall be one flesh."*

~Nathaniel Holcomb
Presiding Bishop
Covenant Connections International, Inc.

Endorsements

Treat Her Like A Lady was written to help men strengthen their marriages and even help those who are preparing for marriage. But this book is also a "must-read" for women, and will help them identify and clarify what they really need from their husbands. Pastor Rob's insights are passionate, practical, and a powerful tool for building strong marriages and family.

~Terri McFaddin-Solomon
Author, Composer, Minister

Treat Her Like A Lady is a must read for every married couple, and for anyone who plans to marry. This book is packed with revelation and wisdom, and is so well written; you will not be able to put it down. I'm a witness!

~Keith Staten
Minister, Psalmist, Songwriter

Introduction

The institution of Marriage today is under severe attack. The divorce rate is deceiving, because even though it is on the decline, more and more couples are living together without "the papers". There is also an increase in same sex relationships cohabitating. Unfortunately, Christian marriages are ending in divorce at as high a rate as any other group in the world. Nevertheless, this comes as no surprise considering the fact that the devil hates the very thing marriage represents; Christ and His church. What is a surprise; however, is the number of Christian homes that are an argument away from disaster, and the husband is seemingly oblivious.

If polled, most husbands can quote Colossians 3:18, which instruct wives to submit unto your own husbands as is fitting in the Lord. Somehow, this scripture, along with Ephesians 5:22 "Wives, submit to your own husbands, as to the Lord", is in every husband's memory verse index. Even unsaved and carnal husbands quote these two scriptures (often on a daily basis).

The question is how many of those same husbands are living Colossians 3:19 which says, **"Husbands, love your wives and do not be bitter toward them?"**

Notice, brothers, we have been instructed not to be bitter toward our wives. In other words, treat her like a lady. The word bitter is defined as not sweet; showing mental pain; resentment, and piercingly cold. It is an oxymoron to call your wife sweetheart and sugar mama, and yet at the same time be bitter towards her.

In the next few chapters, I want to share with you how I found my 'good thing', as well as some practical principles to apply to your marriage that will ensure your 'queen' is Treated Like A Lady.

Table of Contents

Chapter 1: How I Found Her (My Story)..........................1

Chapter 2: Love Her...7

Chapter 3: Locate Her..13

Chapter 4: Learn Her...19

Chapter 5: Listen to Her...27

Chapter 6: Lead Her..33

Chapter 7: Let Her 41

Chapter 8: Lavish Her..47

Resources

Chapter 1

HOW I FOUND HER (MY STORY)

What do you want to be when you grow up? That is the question asked of every child, and I was no exception. However, my answer was not the usual lawyer, doctor, or pro-athlete. I wanted to be a preacher (mama said I was a strange child). Preaching was in my blood. Daddy was a preacher, granddaddy was a preacher, and my uncle was a preacher, not to mention the cousins who were also preachers. I used to mimic our pastor or others I had heard preach. I even taped over Daddy's first sermon with my own sermon. My future was set. I was going to grow up, become a preacher, get married, have a son, and he would grow up and become a preacher. Believe it or not, it almost happened just like that with a few exceptions.

First of all, as I got older, I wasn't so impressed with preachers anymore. It seemed that all they did was 'whoop' or talk like they were professors or something. Most of all, they seemed to do as much sinning as everyone else in the church, or world for that matter. Don't get me wrong, not all of the preachers I knew were that way. As a matter of fact, I was blessed to have a pastor who taught the Word. I must say though, I was convinced that not everyone in the pulpit was called to be there, at least not by God. So, I decided that I wouldn't preach, unless God Himself told me to.

Secondly, along with preaching running in my family, so did divorce. As a matter of fact, there were more divorced than preach-

Robert J. Poole, Jr.

...g. As far back as my great-grandparents, divorce ran rampant on both sides of my family. When I was 11 years old, my parents separated. I was very confused. Daddy was a preacher, but he left momma; he left me. Not long after that, my pastor and his wife divorced. My role models were diminishing right before my eyes. That same year the head deacon of our church divorced his wife. Within about an 18 month span, three men of God I looked up to had all let me down. After that, I told myself I would not get married, until I could afford a divorce. I had concluded that you get married, start a family, and then split up. What a dismal picture.

Years went by. Daddy, my pastor, and the head deacon all remarried. Momma never so much as allowed another man into our home for coffee; I still admire her for that. On the one hand, I thought why even get married, but on the other hand, I thought why not just ask God who to marry, and stay married to her. It was settled; I wasn't going to preach or get married, until God told me to.

At the age of 18, I joined the Army. I took my Bible with me, but I don't think I ever read it; at least not while I was sober. My life had been turned upside down in the course of about three months. I hung with the old 'wine heads', because the guys my age didn't know how to drink. For the next four years of my life, I drank and cursed, and chased women with a vengeance. Thank God for deliverance!

The only exception to my new way of life was when I would come home on leave. All of a sudden, the drinking would stop, the cursing would cease, and I would spend time with my high school sweetheart (who was also cheating). The biggest change was the fact that I was in church every Sunday with that Bible in hand. You see, I couldn't let Momma down; after all, I was going to be a preacher.

Ironically, as soon as leave was over, the party would start all over again. This went on for four years.

My time in the military had ended and so had the party. Now I had a decision to make. Which Robert was going home; the one who would pawn his jewelry to get a half gallon of rum, or the one who would be in church every Sunday. One thing I knew for sure, I could no longer be both.

I'll never forget that drive home. I was leaving Ft. Sill, Oklahoma on my way back to Las Vegas. It was the first serious talk I had with God since I asked Him to explain why Daddy left. I said, "God, I can't keep living this lie. I need you to take the wine, the words, and the women." Somewhere between Albuquerque, New Mexico and Flagstaff, Arizona, I had rededicated my life to the Lord.

When I got home, I ran to the church. I was in church as often as the doors were unlocked. I wanted all God had for me, and I received the baptism with the Holy Spirit on the Friday after Thanksgiving in 1989. It was full speed ahead. I knew I was going to preach God's Word. No more drinking, no more cursing, and no more chasing. As a matter of fact, my pastor appointed me, along with two other brothers, over a young adult Bible study.

I was dating a young lady at church at the time. Now I knew she couldn't be my wife, because I had a glimpse of what God was going to do with me, and she had no intentions of doing those things. So, in my ignorance, I used to pray God would change her, so she would want what I wanted. At the same time, I would pray for my wife that the Lord would keep her and bless her and make me the husband she needed. Mind you, I was still dating this particular young lady, but asking God to bless my future wife.

Brothers, I was a chump! I knew she wasn't my wife, but I wouldn't tell her. I just let her think that one day she would be Mrs. Poole. I was a big chump!

While all of this was going on, I ran into my 'play sister' from high school. We were both at a Benny Hinn meeting. It was wonderful that we were both now serving the Lord. Later that year she called me crying. She was having 'chump' problems, so I went over to comfort my little sister. After that, we would sit up for hours talking about the goodness of the Lord. I thought to myself, this is the kind of woman I would marry. Keep in mind, I didn't even notice her physically; she was my little sister. She decided she was going to move back to Phoenix where she had gotten saved. I knew I would miss her, but she had to do what she felt the Lord had told her to do.

It was March 8, 1992 (my day; everyone else was just existing). A couple of weeks prior to that day, the Lord had me to teach His Word. Now only a few people knew about this, because I wanted confirmation that it was the Lord. Anyway, now it's March 8th, and my little sister is about to leave. She came over to my apartment, and then I followed her back to her place. I gave her fifty dollars, said goodbye, and went to church. A friend of mine was ministering that morning at another church, so I decided I would go and support him. Born and raised in Las Vegas, and I got lost. I couldn't find that church to save my life. So, I decided to go back to my own church. As I walked in, the choir was up singing, so I eased into a pew up front. The pastor came over and whispered to me that the Spirit told him I was to speak that night. Wow! Talk about confirmation. That night I preached my first message to the congregation. Before I knew it, I was back in my apartment. I was still floating; I was officially a preacher. I remember thinking this is the kind of stuff you share with your wife. One problem, I wasn't married. So, I called my little sister in Phoenix. I told her about all that had happened and how the Lord had moved.

SIDEBAR: I must say this; she always tells this part differently from me.

While I'm on the phone sharing with her, as clear as I could hear her, I heard the Spirit of the Lord say to me, "She is your wife." I'm telling you, March 8, 1992 was my day. My first sermon and my wife on the same day; God is awesome! He had honored my childhood dream of being a preacher. More importantly, He spoke directly to me concerning ministry and marriage.

The first person I told was my momma. Then, I called the young lady I had been dating. She came by my apartment the next day. That was the toughest conversation I had ever had; all because I had been a 'chump'. I learned the hard way about dating. Brother if she is not the one, be a man and tell her. Anyway, I still had to teach the Bible study that night. Needless to say, the class was the farthest thing from my mind. I couldn't wait to get back home to call my wife-to-be. The night before, March 8, 1992, we had talked for 9 hours.

Tonight our conversation only went on for about 6 hours. I realized I had never *seen* Sheila as Sheila before. She had always been my little sister. So, I decided to fly to Phoenix to 'see' her. I got off the phone, booked a flight, took a shower, and went to the airport. When I arrived at the Phoenix airport, I didn't see her right away. So, I started walking toward the baggage claim. Breathtaking! She turned the corner wearing a white turtle neck with green hearts on it and green sweats. We were both skinning and grinning the rest of the day. At the very moment I saw her as my wife, the Lord put the love Christ has for the church in me for her. Of course, I didn't know what it was then. All I knew is she was so beautiful.

If someone would have told me growing up that I was going to marry a woman who looked like Sheila, I would have laughed out loud. I'm a tall man, and one of my assumptions was that my wife would be tall like most of my old girlfriends were.

Sheila is only five feet tall and has been that tall (or short) since the ninth grade. None of that mattered when I saw her. All I was thinking was "Wow God, such a pretty lady for me?" When it's God, it doesn't matter if she is pink with blue stripes. He will give you His love for her.

Chapter 2

LOVE HER

In today's society, many words have seemingly taken on new meanings. Some words have become so watered down that they don't have the same impact they once did. For instance, the word gay used to mean lighthearted and carefree, but now it exclusively means a homosexual. Describing something we enjoy has gone from hot to cool; from nice to nasty; from good to bad; from awesome to wicked, and so on. These days, people say I love you, when in actuality they have confused love with lust, or like a lot.

Ephesians 5:25 says **"Husbands, love your wives, even as Christ also loved the church, and gave Himself for it."** What an incredible responsibility we have been given. We have been charged to love our wives the same way Christ loves us! Even though this may seem like a huge request, it's actually quite simple. As a husband, I need look no further than unto Jesus and the way He loves me, and then reciprocate that love to my wife. Before you can love your wife as Christ loves the church, you must first know what love is, as well as what love is not. Remember, the scripture says, "As Christ."

First of all, let's look at what love is not. Love is not lust and love is not like. Lust is the perversion of true love. Like is the subversion of true love. Neither lust nor like can produce what true love can. They are both only mere substitutions of true love.

I have an acronym system to better explain lust and like. Love is not lust. The acronym for **L.U.S.T.** is **Loving Until** you've **Satisfied** your **Temptation**. In other words, you love her as long as you are getting what you want. Men don't have a problem wining and dining a woman, as long as there appears to be something in it for them. Unfortunately, some husbands have the mentality of a boy in high school. Most of us were not trying to get married in high school; we were trying to get a girl to give us what we wanted. Everything from sex to status, we kept her as long as she satisfied our temptations. Once you get married (prayerfully long before) those days are over. You can't keep her as long as she satisfies your wants and then toss her to the side for another. That is not how Christ loves us.

Secondly, love is not like. The acronym for **L.I.K.E.** is **Loving Intimacy Kindled Emotions**. You don't really love her; you just enjoy the way you feel when you are with her. You would rather go to the movies with her than with your cousin. She is your preferred cook or your choice of companion. As your wife, she must be more than just the one you like to be with. There are some men who see their wife as just another thing to do on the list. They enjoy her company, but only when they want to be cozy. I call it the Saturday night love; because that's the only time she knows you love her. Why? You **L**ove the **I**ntimacy **K**indled **E**motions. If she says no to Saturday night, you begin to look elsewhere for intimacy. That is not the way Christ loves us.

In the Bible, there are several Greek words for the word love. There is *phileo* love, which is friendship love. *Phileo* is the type of love one has for a friend or acquaintance. *Phileo* love says, "I'm fond of you." The next love is *storge*; which is best known as family love. *Storge* is the love that says blood is thicker than water. *Storge* is the love siblings have for one another. Thirdly, there is *eros* love, which is feeling love. *Eros* is where the word erotic derives from. This love is the one in which the enemy perverts most. *Eros* is physical love, and should be only experienced between a husband and wife. Finally, there is *agape* love. *Agape* love is the Father's love. *Agape* love is the love husbands are commanded to love their wives with, according to Ephesians 5:25. *Agape* is known as the love of choice.

Although all four of these loves are experienced in a marriage, we need to understand that agape is the more excellent way. My wife is my best friend, and I am fond of her, but my love does not stop there. She is bone of my bone and flesh of my flesh; however, she is more than family to me. She is a vision of beauty to me, and I so enjoy her touch, yet, she means so much more to me than someone to hold in the night. I love her with the love of choice; with the love in which Christ loves me.

First Corinthians 13: 4–7 from the Message Bible reads, "**Love never gives up. Love cares more for others than for self. Love doesn't want what it doesn't have. Love doesn't strut, doesn't have a swelled head, doesn't force itself on others, isn't always 'me first', doesn't fly off the handle, doesn't keep score of the sins of others, doesn't revel when others grovel, takes pleasure in the flowering of truth, puts up with anything, trusts God always, always looks for the best, never looks back, but keeps on going to the end. Love never dies.**"

The love of choice, or the love with which Christ loves us, is agape. The acronym for **AGAPE** is **Always Giving Above Personal Expectations.** AGAPE always puts the one it loves before itself. Agape is the God-kind of love. Unfortunately, many husbands don't **AGAPE** their wives, but rather **AGATPE**. The acronym for **AGATPE** is **Always Giving According To Personal Expecta-**

tions. The only time she is treated like a lady is when you feel like she's done a good job. Don't keep tabs on her shortcomings. Christ gives above His personal expectation of us. When we fall short, He loves us up.

God is a covenant-making, covenant-keeping God. The scriptures tell us that God is love. Therefore, His love is a covenant-love (everlasting). You must love your wife and see your marriage as a covenant. When in covenant, your primary goal is the one you are in covenant with. That is why we are always on God's mind and in His heart, because He is in covenant-love with us.

Some men, instead of a covenant marriage, have a convenient marriage. Convenience means suitable, freedom from discomfort. I call it the 7/11 marriage, because as long as it is convenient, they are in it. As soon as things get tough, they get going. When the rains descend and the winds blow, convenience is altered. When the babies come or the bills start rolling in that is not the time to check out. Remember, convenience always costs more. Leaving her because it is no longer convenient will cost you more in the long run (alimony, child support) than staying. The problem with convenience stores is that there is always another one a little bigger offering a little more(i.e. 7/11 versus Walgreens.)

There used to be a 7/11 on just about every corner. It was never meant to replace the supermarket; it was simply there when you needed it. They only sold a fraction of what the supermarkets sold, and they sold it for more than it would cost at a full sized grocery store. All of a sudden, you started seeing fewer 7/11's, and began to see more Walgreens'. These new-style convenience stores offered more than 7/11, but they still didn't have as much as a supermarket. Even though Walgreens can't replace the supermarket, they've reduced 7/11 to Slurpees and Big Gulps. I can't remember the last time I bought something other than a soft drink or candy from a 7/11, because now on every corner there is a Walgreens. Just like I left 7/11 for Walgreens, so are most men who marry for convenience much more likely to take flight when something a little better comes along.

Some brothers have a contract marriage. A contract is a binding agreement between two or more parties to protect ones self and properties. I refer to this as the 50/50 marriage. The 50/50 marriage is where you hear the husband say, "I did my part!" Rather than go the extra mile to make the marriage work, they go a few miles down the road to divorce court. In marriage, your part is not half, it's all. There will be times when you are going to need to do more than your share. Marriage is not 50/50; marriage is 0 thru 100. It is a continuum. The goal is not doing my part; it's all getting done. The objective is doing whatever it takes to get the job done. When your wife is carrying your baby, for example, you need to do more than usual; sometimes you may need to do it all. Christ is not our part-time Savior, Healer, and Supplier; He is all that we need all the time. As long as you have a contract mindset, breaching is a possibility, because contracts are always being renegotiated, amended, and even broken. Don't look for a way out of your marriage.

SIDEBAR: Your marriage isn't some lease agreement waiting to be broken. Christ didn't lease you! Selah!

When we see marriage as a covenant, it changes everything. A covenant is more than a contract, and it is not established or kept based upon convenience. Covenant is God talk. A covenant is also a binding agreement between two or more parties; however, it's established to protect the rights of the other party. In other words, I die to my rights in order to establish the rights of the one I am in covenant with. The best way for me to describe the marriage covenant is on the wedding day; both groom and bride should be escorted down the aisle by pallbearers. Why, because both should enter into the union D.O.A. (dead on arrival). When both are dead to themselves, then they can live for one another.

According to apostolic order, as a husband, my wife is second only to God. I didn't say should be, I said she *is*. Whatever you hold dearest or love the most is what/whom you are married to. Your wife may have the ring, but does something or someone else have your heart? Some men are married to their careers. Others are married to their friends, family, or even themselves.

As a pastor, I see first-hand brothers in ministry married to the ministry. The church is Christ's wife not mine. When I stand before God, He is not going to ask me if I loved His church. He's going to ask me to give account as to how I treated His daughter. It is a pathetic sight when a wife is competing with the church for her husband's affection. Since God is not into wife sharing, why are you showing more interest in His wife than in the one He gave you? It's simple; you take care of your wife, and let God take care of His.

Can you fathers imagine how sickening you would feel if your daughter was being mistreated by her husband? Try to imagine explaining to your Heavenly Father why you said what you said or did what you did to His daughter! That's right, she may be your wife, but she is His daughter. With that in mind, you probably want to ensure you Treat Her Like a Lady.

If you love your job, your church, or even your Momma more than your wife, repent and ask the Holy Spirit to help you *A.G.A.P.E.* her.

Chapter 3

LOCATE HER

In the last chapter, we looked at the right way to love our wives. Yet, in order to love your wife the right way, you must ensure that she is in the right place. Think of it this way, what good are reading glasses to you when you are trying to read if they are in your pocket? The problem isn't the glasses; they are more than sufficient to help you read better. The problem is the glasses are in the wrong place. As your help meet, your wife is more than sufficient to help you do what you are doing better. All too often, she is in the wrong place.

I'm sure you have heard the saying that behind every good man is a good woman. Some would argue that beside every good man is a good woman. The truth of the matter is that both statements are correct. Sheila stands beside me, because we are joint heirs. Notwithstanding, she also stands behind me, because she has my back. She not only stands with me, but she also looks out for wolves that might attack from the rear. Unfortunately, some brothers don't have a clue as to where their wife is. They aren't sure if she is beside, behind, or even leading. If you don't know where she is, how can she help you?

In 1 Corinthians 11:3 the Bible says, "**But I want you to know that the head of every man is Christ, the head of woman is man and the head of Christ is God.**" Verse 7 says, "**For a man indeed ought not to cover his head, since he is the image and glory of God; but woman is the glory of man.**"

It has been said that moon rock is one of the dullest rocks known to man. Nevertheless, what makes moon rock so unique is its ability to reflect light. The moon has no light of its own, yet reflects the sun so well that it lights up the night. The moon's radiance is merely the reflection of the sun's brilliance. When there is nothing blocking the moon from the sun, the moon is full. The moon is the glory of the sun.

You are the sun and your wife is the moon. She is your glory! She can only shine to the degree of the amount of light reflecting off of her. If your wife is not glowing, something has come between the two of you and/or between you and God. The only other reason she would not be shining is if she is leading you. Don't allow your marriage to become one where you are not even seen because you have been eclipsed by your wife. God made you the head. Get in place and shine on your queen. You must make it your business not to allow anything or anyone come between you and your wife; not your job, family, or ministry. Where is she? Is she glowing?

I once read where a well known man of God said that before he comes to any conclusion about another man, he must first meet that man's wife. If the wife is dry, depressed, and dreary, the husband is not doing his job. On the other hand, if the wife is joyful, jovial, and glowing, the husband is in the right place.

I hear men complain about their wives that she is this and that…she never…she always…and so on. Most of them get a little bothered when I tell them that she is only reflecting them. As you reflect Christ to your wife, she can't help but reflect Christ. She can't help but be happy, cheerful, and pleasant. She can't help but glow with the radiance of God's love. Yes, your wife's relationship with the Lord is between her and the Lord. However, ask yourself how much of her glow is because of you. If you can honestly say your wife is not shining the way you would like, locate her, so that you can remove the blockage.

The definition of locate is to discover the place of; to detect or identify. Men, you cannot locate what you do not pay attention to. All too often husbands miss the subtle hints of the wife and don't notice, until alarms are sounding. Did you notice that she cooked your favorite meal? Did you notice her new dress? Did you notice that she's been slimming down? By the way, let me help you. If you notice all of these things about her, but you don't compliment her, you are only fueling her complaint of you! And the sisters said, "Amen!"

SIDEBAR: The more you compliment; the less she will complain.

Proverbs 5:15 says, "**Drink water from your own cistern, and running water from your own well**". It goes on to say in verse 19, "**As a loving deer and a graceful doe, let her breasts satisfy you at all times; and always be enraptured with her love.**"

You may be wondering "what does this have to do with locating my wife?" Brother, why do you think she is trying to lose weight? Why do you think she is wearing a new hair style? She is trying to get you to take notice of her. Selah!

The number of married women having plastic surgery is escalating every year. They are going through all of the tucks, pulls, and implants to get their husbands to still be attracted to them. As men of God, there should be no question about our physical attraction to our wives. Unfortunately, *in the church*, men are leaving their wives for younger versions; trading their wives in, as it were, on newer improved models. Many men are giving up their precious, priceless prize in exchange for a plastic, polished, trophy wife. We have given the enemies of God great occasion to blaspheme God.

I remember when the two-seater Thunderbird made a comeback. At first, it appeared as though Ford had out done itself. They had given the original a make over, and added some modern features with just enough of the original look to catch your eye. However, after just a little time, they realized that the new version, with all of its bells and whistles, still did not compare to the original T-bird. The new T-bird costs more, but was actually worth less than the original T-bird in mint condition. The key is keeping the original version in mint condition. In other words, the original will always be more valuable if it is taken care of as priceless in the first place. In reality, those who know cars know it is not how new the vehicle is as much as it is how diligent the owner takes care of the vehicle.

All of the bells and whistles in the world can't replace heartfelt TLC.

Did you marry for shape or substance? Some people like the shape of the cola bottle more than the cola itself. If you really enjoy cola, it doesn't matter to you if it is in a bottle, can, or 2 liter container. Why? Because you want what's inside of the container more than the container itself. When you make your wife feel guilty or condemned about the weight she has gained (more than likely from having your babies) you are telling her you are more interested in the bottle's shape than its content. This is why so many men marry a younger woman the second time around. They are trying to remarry the wife of their youth, as though they are still a young man.

I see Sheila as a living epistle inspired by God. The more I notice her, the more I see what He has given me. It's like a fresh revelation every time I behold her. Practically speaking, the one looking always sees more than the one being looked at. I've discovered that when I notice Sheila, she becomes more noticeable. If I say to her, "You look very nice in that color." Next thing I know, she is wearing that color more and more. Now that I've noticed her, she wants to be noticed all the more.

Man of God, locate your wife and begin to see just how blessed you are to have your queen. Begin to reflect on the way she walks or the way she says your name. Think about how pretty she is and what her smile does to you. Now, right now! Go tell her how much you love her. Tell her how grateful you are to God for giving you the awesome honor of being her husband. Don't just look at her outward beauty. Pull out her inward beauty; tell her how beautiful her spirit is.

Chapter 4

LEARN HER

Many husbands are frustrated in their marriage, because they feel they just cannot seem to figure out their wife. Some even go so far as to say, 'I'll never understand my wife.' Hold up man, you have been commanded to know, or understand her.

First Peter 3:7 reads, **"Husbands, likewise dwell with them with understanding, giving honor to the wife, as the weaker vessel, and being heirs together of the grace of life, that your prayers may not be hindered."**

Listen to that same verse from the New Living Translation:

"In the same way, you husbands must give honor to your wives. Treat her with understanding as you live together. She may be weaker than you are, but she is your equal partner in God's gift of new life. If you don't treat her as you should, your prayers will not be heard." Please note, you are not commanded to understand women, just your wife. I think this is vital to the success of any marriage. For some reason, brothers attempt to treat their wife the way they treated their high school sweetheart or some old flame they would not have married anyway. Though a woman, your wife can't be so easily generalized. She is as unique as you are. Remember, all women are not the same. What works for my father in the faith and his queen may not work for me and mine. Flowers may not be the answer for you. You must have some knowledge of the woman you are married to.

So what does it mean to dwell with knowledge or understanding? Knowledge means awareness or familiarity of a person, fact, or thing. It is a person's range of information or the sum of what is known. Simply put, it means to know your wife and treat her accordingly; something as simple as knowing her favorite color or her idea of a romantic evening. Does she like going out or does she prefer to spend her evenings at home?

Sheila, by her own admission, is a delicate flower. In other words, she is dainty and elegant. She doesn't open doors. She doesn't pump gas. She doesn't kill bugs. She doesn't change light bulbs. She refuses to participate in any activity that may lead to the breaking of a fingernail; and I love her for it! I have peace in my home, because I **know** how she is. I'm a wise man. Proverbs 1:5 says, "**A wise man will hear and increase in learning, and a man of understanding will attain wise counsel.**" The way I see it, if God values the marriage union so much to the extent He considers the church His Son's wife, I had better make it my business to understand mine.

When you think about it, we have the awesome privilege and responsibility to love our wives the same way Christ loves us. That said, it would behoove us to make sure we do our job well. Even now, I ask myself what I can do to understand my wife better than I already do. Please hear me, the only way you can learn her is to spend time with her Creator and with her.

Studies show that it takes about five years to really get to know your spouse. Sad to say, however, most marriages end within the first three years. Thus, most people divorce someone they never even got to know. God wants you to know your wife.

I hear so many husbands complain how their wife has changed. I tell them the woman I'm married to is not the same woman I married. Change is good! My wife is more secure. She is more confident in who she is. She is more and more like Jesus. I thank God she is not the same woman I married. I really thank God I am not the same man she married!

Before you slander her for changing, investigate if her change isn't in reality growth. Could it be that she has grown spiritually and you haven't? After all, the average Christian woman spends more time in prayer than her husband. She spends more time in the Word than her husband. No wonder she's changed, she's been with the Lord more.

Brothers, it is imperative that you spend quality time alone with the Lord. The more time you spend in prayer and the Word, the more He can reveal to you how to know His jewel He gave you. Please don't say you will never understand your wife. Jesus would have never told us to love her the way He loves us if it were not possible to do so. Jesus has never told the Father that He doesn't understand His church.

Hebrews 4:15 in the Message Bible reads, **"We don't have a priest who is out of touch with our reality. He's been through weakness and testing, experienced it all – all but the sin."** In other words, our High Priest can relate. He's in touch with our feelings (emotions).

I hear men say, "My wife is too emotional and I'm just not an emotional person." Anger is an emotion most men don't seem to have a problem understanding. Maybe you need to get in touch with your emotional side to better understand her emotions. Whatever you have to do, you can't use the excuse, 'I don't get her'; after all, she came out of you.

The Word of God will help you if you look in it for help.

Deuteronomy 24:5 says, **"When a man has taken a wife, he shall not go to war or be charged with any business; he shall be free at home one year, and bring happiness to his wife whom he has taken."**

What an incredible verse of scripture! God commanded the man to stay at home for a whole year. Can you imagine taking a one year honeymoon? The sole purpose of doing so is to bring happiness to your wife. God has charged us to take the time to make our wives happy.

The King James Version of the Bible uses the word 'cheer', instead of 'bring happiness'. The word cheer means to make glad or cause to rejoice. The question is do you bring your wife cheer or fear? Is she eagerly anticipating your arrival or anxiously awaiting your departure? Have you given her reasons to be cheerful or fearful? Why is she happy? Why is she sad? Why is she crying? Has she been sending you a signal that you've been ignoring? Ignoring is more than just not knowing; it is refusing to take notice.

I realize that in today's economy it is near impossible for someone to take an entire year off from work and not end up homeless. Nevertheless, you can still make a point to have a date night or perhaps a quarterly get away.

As you may already know, the divorce rate in the United States is around 65%, meaning 2 out 3 marriages will not make it. However, you may not know that the divorce rate among those who consistently take vacations is only 10%. What does that say about making time to spend with your wife? The more time you spend with her (without distractions), the more you will want to make a lifetime of it!

SIDEBAR: Church functions (convocations, conferences, revival meetings, and so on) ARE NOT VACATIONS!

So go on and plan that vacation. Stop making excuses as to why you can't take one. You've got to make the time. You may not be able to take her on a 7 day cruise, but you can at least take her on a 2 day get away. Is she not worth it?

God, in His infinite wisdom, created a way to get away everyday. It is called the garden. The Bible says that Adam and his wife heard the voice of the Lord God walking in the garden in the cool of the day (Genesis 3:8a).

I believe this was God's daily routine. This is the place God created for intimacy. It is the place where one can be naked and not ashamed (Genesis 2:25). This is the place where God could come and be with His creation without distraction and His creation could come to Him without any shame or fear.

As it relates to marriage, I believe we too must have a place of intimacy. Sheila and I refer to that place as the garden. It is where we can be naked and not ashamed. For us, the garden is our bedroom, a.k.a. the throne room. How I look forward to meeting her there, nightly. It's in the garden, where I'm not dad or pastor; I'm just Robert. It is there where we have 'pillow talk'.

"Pillow talk" is our phrase for intimate conversation about our day or whatever, without distraction. It is in our garden where we learn more about each other. We learn more about each others' likes and dislikes. We learn more about each others' weaknesses and strengths. And because it's the garden, we are free to be open to one another without fear of being exposed to others.

I must add this in. As important as it is to spend quality garden time with your wife, you must first spend garden time with God. Selah! Getting to know your wife better without getting to know God better for the most part isn't better at all. Why? Without God in my marriage, regardless of how well Sheila and I get along, it would be useless.

The best way to explain it is to look at the illustration below:

As you can see, the closer the two of you get to God, the closer you get to one another. If you continue to just get closer to one another on a horizontal plain (according to the flesh), neither of you will be any closer to Him. Even in marriage, it's all about Him! When you pursue Him daily and she pursues Him daily, you both come closer together, daily.

Sheila and I can tell when one of us has not spent time with the Lord. We are cranky, crabby, and cross with each other. At first, this would lead to us nearly arguing over the smallest of things.

Now, that we've been at this a while, we quickly recognize that we got our day started together before we started with the Lord. Basically, regardless of how much time Sheila and I spend together, if we don't first spend time with God, the best we can offer each other is our flesh. The closer we get to God individually; the closer we are together, jointly. As I pursue Jesus and Sheila pursues Jesus, we see more of Him in one another; which makes us want to chase each other. Selah!

Chapter 5

LISTEN TO HER

The easiest way to get an answer is to ask a question. On the other hand, one of the hardest things for a man to do is ask for help. Swallow your pride, my brother; you don't know everything.

When Sheila and I counsel couples, the overwhelmingly biggest complaint of the wife is communication. Either the husband doesn't listen to her, or they never talk. When we ask the husband, his response usually is, "I talk, but she doesn't listen to me." What a sad commentary to know Christian homes are falling apart because of a lack of communication.

First of all, communication involves more listening than talking. Jesus often would say, "He that has an ear let him hear." The problem is too many of us have an opinion, not an ear. Therefore, communication in the home is redefined.

We spend more time trying to explain what we are saying than we do listening to the other person.

A soft answer turns away wrath, but a harsh word stirs up anger (Proverbs 15:1). When we engage in conversation with someone, we do one of three things: a) we talk at; b) we talk to; or c) we talk with. Let's look at these one at a time.

First of all, we have talking at someone. I refer to talking at someone as barking. Some Christian homes look more like a zoo than heaven. The husband is barking. The wife is quacking. The son is hissing to warn visitors they are entering a war zone. The baby sounds like a parrot saying, "Awk, mom is stupid, mom is stupid, awk." Turn it down a few octaves. Remember, it is a soft answer that turns away wrath. Once I've raised my voice, I'm no longer interested in anything but my point of view. I'm right and therefore you must be wrong. Consequently, I'm talking at you, because as far as I'm concerned, only what I say matters.

Secondly, we have talking to someone. I refer to talking to someone as teaching. When talking to someone I am trying to help them. For example, I talk to my son more often than not, because I'm trying to help him understand what I already know. When I am ministering the Word of God to my congregation, I am talking to them, because I am instructing them in the Word. When talking to someone, I am interested in their opinion, but I'm trying to get them to understand mine. Many husbands make the error of attempting to teach their wife how to be a wife. You can't teach someone to be what you have never been, unless you are an instructor in that field. Trust me; we husbands have not been trained in training our wives. Selah!

Finally, we have talking with someone. This is the highest form of communication, because both parties are sharing. Talking with someone is also the most vulnerable form of communication, because I am giving the one I'm talking with permission to speak into my life. This is why prayer is considered talking with God. In prayer, we allow the Father to speak into our life at the expense of making changes, if necessary. Just as true prayer begins with listening to God, so it is when talking with your wife. When I'm talking with my wife, not only does she share her heart, but I, in turn, share mine. Truthfully, a lot of brothers don't want to hear what's in their wife's heart. Because most men don't want to know they are not always right.

Try talking with your wife instead of barking at her. Turn the volume down. Begin talking with her, instead of trying to instruct her on how to be her. She is not trying out for the team and you are not her coach! The Word of God is here to help us improve in our communication skills. In James 1:19, 20 the Word says, "**So then, my beloved brethren, let every man be swift to hear, slow to speak, slow to wrath; for the wrath of man does not produce the righteousness of God.**"

I thought it interesting that hearing is listed before speaking. Most are in such a rush to voice their view; they never hear their wife's view on the matter. If you do not first hear, how will you know the best way to answer? Be slow to speak. Don't be in such a hurry to prove your point, that you cut her off mid-sentence. God knows I can use some help in that area. Let her finish talking, so you can respond properly, instead of reacting hastily and harshly.

I have found saying I'm sorry does wonders. In order to keep peace, just apologize. You may say I did apologize, but she won't forgive me. It could be she has forgiven you, she just doesn't trust you. Forgiveness is instant. However, it takes time to rebuild trust. Something I call the trust factor.

I can recall, while living in Saint Louis, Missouri, we were out shopping. Our routine was grabbing something to eat between stores. This particular time, while driving, I was trying to finish my burger before we got to the next store. Needless to say, I rear-ended another car; it was a simple fender-bender (Joshua and Shekinah didn't even wake up), but Sheila was traumatized. After that, whenever she saw red lights in front of us, regardless to how far away, she would press down as hard as she could on the imaginary brake on the passenger side. This literally went on for years.

I would get so frustrated, because I had apologized seemingly a thousand times. Then the Lord spoke to me. He said to me, "It isn't that she hasn't forgiven you; she doesn't trust your driving." What a revelation! Sheila just needed time to regain trust in my driving again. So, I began to pray that God would remove all fear that I had caused in her due to my driving. Trust is like the human body. If it is broken or injured, it immediately begins to heal. Even so, the length of healing is predicated on the damage done to it.

I praise God that in the 15 years Sheila and I have been married, we have never argued; even during times of rebuilding trust. I didn't say we have never disagreed or had moments of silence (sometimes hours or days), but we have never argued.

We have disagreed with one another, but we have never disrespected one another. I've never raised my voice at her or belittled her with my words. Why? Jesus has never raised His voice at me or belittled me with His Word. Don't forget, brothers, He is our example of how to treat our wives. Why do you have to be right? Why does she have to be wrong? In reality, it doesn't matter who is right or wrong, it's all about Him, not us.

Sometimes Sheila sounds just like God. I'm not always right and she is definitely not always wrong. I had to learn to listen to my wife, because for the most part, she is only saying to me what God would say. I know men who refuse to make a move in their home, finances, and even ministry if the suggestion came from their wives. At the same time, those same brothers will risk nearly everything, because someone else (often one who does not even have their best interest at heart) makes a suggestion. God forbid they say they have heard the Lord.

If you would learn to listen to your wife, you would find that the Lord is confirming through her what He's already spoken to you. Listening to what she is saying and how she is saying it will help you gain insight on how to say what's in your heart or on your mind.

I once heard a preacher ask, 'Can you handle the truth?' Now before you answer, think about the question again. Most men have no problem telling the truth, regardless of how brutal. Husbands tell me all the time, all I did was tell her she needed to lose some weight or something like that. Before you go telling her she's gaining weight, look in the mirror. Is there now a keg where a six pack of abs used to be? Can you handle her telling you she wishes she could see your waist? Can you handle her telling you she doesn't want to go and visit your mother this Thanksgiving? Has your wife been lying to you, because she knows you can't handle the truth? Does she know that you will bark at her if she were to be as brutally honest with you as you are with her?

In Proverbs 15:1, we saw it is a soft answer that turns away wrath. Verse 2 of that same chapter says, **"The tongue of the wise uses knowledge rightly, but the mouth of fools pours out foolishness."** In other words, it's all in the way you say it.

If your wife is complaining about the way she looks, buying her a treadmill is not the answer! Use wisdom. Don't say something cold like you need to work out or join the gym. Rely on what I call righteous rap. The Holy Ghost got game! Regrettably, some brothers got saved and stupid all at the same time. For example, you remember how you used to lay your 'mack' on the ladies in high school.

    Take her for a romantic walk in the park (about a mile long). When you are finished walking, tell her the sweat on her brow is doing something to you. Then suggest to her that the two of you do this at least two to three times a week; maybe even at a brisker pace, because her sweat is like the dew of Mt. Hermon. Tell her how you can't wait to get her home, so you can run her a hot bath and allow the steam from the tub to cause her entire body to sweat. If you're really tough, you can say something like the steam from the bath can't compare to the passion burning inside of you.

    It's all in the way you say it!

Chapter 6

LEAD HER

As the husband, you have been given the task of being the priest of your home, the king of the castle; the man of the house. Most men will not hesitate to reiterate to all other persons involved who the boss is. Ironically, in many homes, the husband is not living up to his self-proclaimed title(s).

In Genesis chapter 1, we find the creation of man. In Genesis chapter 2, we find the instruction to man. Finally, in Genesis chapter 3, we find the fall of man. I want to focus in on chapter 3, because this is where many marriages are. Now, before you jump to conclusions, let me explain.

In Genesis 2:16 and 17, God gives clear instructions to the man. As a matter of fact, the scripture says the Lord commanded the man. However, in chapter three, the serpent is talking to the woman. Unfortunately, the sisters have been given a bad reputation ever since. I'm not talking to or about sisters, I'm talking to the man of the house. Before you go and stone the woman for her conversation with the serpent, let me give you some rock-dropping truth.

First of all, why didn't Adam say anything? Some have taught that Adam was not there during this devilish conversation. Oh but that is not the case. The Bible says she gave to her husband **with** her. Adam was there with her, or at least close enough to see and hear what was taking place all along. The reason Adam was quiet is because though he was the head, he did not lead. Adam gave up his rights as the head and let his wife handle it. He ~~wore~~ the crown of the king, but the queen reigned.

SIDEBAR : There can be no Jezebel without an Ahab!

"Now the serpent was more cunning or subtle than any other beast…" (Genesis 3:1). Genesis 2:19, 20 says, **"Out of the ground the Lord God formed every beast of the field and every bird of the air, and brought them to Adam to see what he would call them. And whatever Adam called each living creature that was its name. So Adam gave names to all cattle, to the birds of the air, and to every beast of the field. But for Adam there was not found a helper comparable to him."**

According to this passage, Adam named all of the animals. I believe he named them according to their character. In other words, Adam did not name the Ox an ox and it ***began*** to act like an ox. He named it an ox ***because*** it acted like an ox. Adam was so in tune to God that he called the animals by the name God would have called them. Adam wasn't suggesting to God, "How about we call this one a gerbil?" He called the gerbil a gerbil, because that was the heart of God for that particular animal.

This leads me to my next question. Why did Adam allow his wife to talk to the serpent in the first place? As soon as the serpent began to converse with the woman, he should have stepped in, if for no other reason than it was the serpent. Adam was fully aware of the subtle craftiness of the serpent, because he is the one who named it. Adam sat back and let his woman handle it. Although this is not scripture, I believe when the serpent first approached the woman, she looked at her husband. And because of his silence, she felt she had to take action.

Many homes today resemble this picture. Being cognizant of the bill collectors and telemarketers, some husbands sit back and leave their wives to deal with those serpents. Many wives are left to handle the bills, the meals, and the deals. She has to make sure all of the bills are paid. She has to make sure all of the meals are on the table. She also has to deal with the post office, dry cleaners, auto mechanic, and so on.

Even as it relates to the children, the wife is often left to raise them on her own. All the while, the 'king of the castle' is seated on his throne a.k.a. lazy-boy, with his scepter, a.k.a. remote-control, in hand, refusing to be bothered with such paltry duties. The king has delegated decision-making to the queen. Every decision from where to go on vacation, to what church to join is left up to the wife.

Unfortunately, more and more young men are being raised in single parent homes. In most cases, that parent is the mother. As a teenager, when a young man needs his dad the most, my mom was thrust into the role of single parent (via divorce). I praise God my momma raised me to be a man. So often, single moms spoil and pamper their sons. When that boy becomes a man, he is so used to getting his way, he marries his momma. In other words, he marries the first woman that will allow him to continue to be a spoiled brat. Since his momma fixed him breakfast in bed, he expects his wife to do the same. All he had to worry about in his momma's house was not getting someone pregnant.

So now, he expects his wife to be 'Maggie the maid', and jump at his every call.

I believe, (I stress, I believe) many mothers ruin their sons, because he becomes the man in their life. Since the father has walked out, the mom pampers the son in an effort to make sure he never walks out on her. While her little man gets whatever he wants, mom trains the daughter for single-hood survival. The daughter is constantly being reminded to get a good education and make something of herself, because no one is going to take care of her but her. So, the daughter grows up with a spirit of independence, which often leads to unwillingness to submit in marriage. The son on the other hand, develops a spirit of dependence, and therefore struggles to lead his home. He finds himself needing his wife; leading from behind. He becomes hesitant in decision making and eventually, he stops making any at all.

In many homes the king's royal decree is, "Ask your mother!" Your daughter asks if she can go to the party, even though it's a school night and you say, "Ask your mother." Your daughter asks if she can sleep over her girlfriend's house and you say, "Ask your mother." Your daughter asks if can go to the movies with her girlfriend's brother and you say, "Ask your mother." She asks if she can go camping with her girlfriend's 'family' and once again you say, "Ask your mother." She tells you, "Dad, I'm pregnant", and you say, "Ask your mother… WHAT?" It is a little late to be dad now. You've been there all along, but abdicating your kingly duties to the queen.

Brothers, we have been called to lead our homes. Don't surrender your responsibilities to your wife. You married your wife; you did not hire her. Stop treating her like a maid. The Bible says she is your helper, not your servant.

You have to not just be the **man** of the house; you must be the **band** of the house. The band of the house or house-band is where we get the word husband from. The house-band is the steward of his home, keeping everything in tact. True house-bands don't rule their home as much as they 'run' their home. They 'run' the vacuum, they 'run' the dishwasher, they 'run' the washer and dryer; they 'run' their home!

I am a firm believer that if you would learn to 'run' your home more, your wife would have more energy to run you around the house! My goal is to free Sheila from as much as possible, in order to ensure she's never too tired. Selah! Use some wisdom and help your helper with the energy zapping chores (homework, cleaning, etc.), so she won't have to tell you not tonight, I'm too tired.

Let me interject here before we go on to the next chapter. It is most difficult to lead your wife if you don't leave your family.

Genesis 2:24 says, "**Therefore a man shall leave his father and his mother and be joined to his wife, and they shall become one flesh**."

First you must leave family and allow her to be your family. It is men who leave; boys stay home. You don't need to run by your parent's house every day. You don't have to celebrate every holiday at your Momma's house. Your wife is now your primary focus.

Secondly, you must cleave. It is very hard to cleave unto your wife when you bowl on Tuesday, play softball on Thursday, have boys' night out on every other Friday, and watch football all day Saturday. It never ceases to amaze me how men wait until they are grown to want to act like boys. When you were in high school trying to be a man by chasing the girls, you should have been hanging with the boys. Now that you are a man, you don't have time to chase your wife, because you are always hanging with the boys. Something is wrong with that picture.

I'm not telling you to retire from your athletic ventures, but you must find the balance. In cleaving, it is imperative that you learn to compromise with your wife. The two are becoming one. Only in marriage is compromise absolutely necessary in order for the two of you to become one! She is not to become your flesh nor are you to become her flesh. The two of you are to become one flesh. I said all of that to say, something has got to give. If you're going to continue playing all of these sports, make sure she is in agreement with you. If she doesn't mind, praise the Lord. Just be careful, because time spent on the field is time lost with your wife.

With that in mind, it leads me to weaving. In Ecclesiastes chapter four, Solomon says two are better than one. Verse twelve says, **"Though one may be overpowered by another, two can withstand him. And a threefold cord is not easily broken."**

It has been said that the strongest cord is a threefold cord, because all three strands of the cord equally touch one another. As soon as another strand is added to the cord it is weakened, because the cords are no longer able to all equally touch each other. The marriage cord is comprised of God, husband, and wife. Once anyone or anything else is added (i.e. momma, ministry, children, etc.), the cord is weakened.

For instance, picture God, your wife, and you as three cords holding hands in a circle. Each one of you has an equal portion of each other. The only way to let a fourth cord in, is to let go of either God or your wife. Unfortunately, many couples have so many cords in their rope that they are no longer touching God or their spouse.

Men of God; leave, cleave, and weave! This is not a suggestion to abandon your family. Once you are married, your priorities change. Your parents and siblings are still your family, but they are not as important as your wife. Your love for them doesn't change, but it doesn't compare, and should not compete with the love you have for your wife. You cannot allow anyone to weaken your bond between you, your wife, and the Lord. You don't owe anyone an explanation; you're only obeying the scriptures.

Go on and lead her by example and ensample. Be determined that she will not love the Lord anymore than you. You rise early and pray over your family. You spend quality time with the Lord. Allow God to lead you in leading her.

Chapter 7

LET HER

Men are proud by nature. Most of us men won't ask for directions, at least not with the intentions of following them. Often, the only instructions we will follow is the picture on the box of whatever we are putting together. As long as we have a hammer and some duct tape, we can fix anything. You know there is something around your house that you've added a couple of nails to or a strip or two of duct tape, in order to make it work. That is what we do; we are fixers. If it's broken, we fix it. There is just one problem; we did not marry an appliance. Our wives can't be fixed with a hammer or a roll of duct tape.

I want to help you, so you are not getting unnecessary grey hair over your inability to fix your wife. Stop trying to fix your wife! You were asleep when the Lord made her. God never told you to fix your wife, just love her.

Genesis 2:21-22 says, "**And the Lord God caused a deep sleep to fall on Adam, and he slept; and He took one of his ribs, and closed up the flesh in its place. Then the rib which the Lord God had taken from man He made into a woman, and He brought her to the man.**"

Brothers are frustrated and aggravated with their wives, because they cannot seem to 'fix' her problems. Since you were asleep, the simple solution is to ask the One who never sleeps or slumbers for help. I know help is a four letter word for some men, but if you want her to be happy, ask God for help.

When Sheila and I were first married, she would cry all the time (what a blow to my male ego). I had no idea what was wrong, but I knew I had to fix it.

SIDEBAR: Duct tapping her eyes shut will not stop the tears.

After many months of wondering what would stop the tears, I broke down and asked God for help. Actually, I asked God to make her stop crying so much. His answer was not exactly what I wanted to hear. He said to me, "If you want her to stop crying, let her cry." I thought to myself, 'Let her cry? That's the problem.' God said, "No, the problem is you are trying to fix her, but you didn't make her. All I need you to do is love her and let her." What a revelation! God never intended for me to make Sheila become what I want. He created her to become what He wants. I realized the more I encouraged Sheila to be herself, the more helpful she became to me fulfilling my destiny. Instead of fixing her problem, I let her be herself without any guilt or condemnation for not being perfect.

Now, I must warn you, brothers, if you are going to let her be herself, there will be times she will not agree with you. Since she is free to be herself, you must learn to agree to disagree. In other words, learn how to disagree without disrespecting. She is your wife, not your daughter. You can't send her to her room or put her on restriction when she doesn't agree with you. You can't take her toys from her, because she spoke her mind.

Some wives are treated as though they are on house arrest. They can not leave home without permission. If they are gone too long or too far, their ankle bracelet begins to alarm. They can't talk on the phone without permission. If they are on the phone too long your pre-recorded message comes on reminding her she only has thirty seconds before the phone automatically ends the call. Some can't even go to church without permission. It's as if they are hoping to be paroled for good behavior. God wants you Pharaohs, I mean husbands, to let His daughters go. Your wife must be free to be who God made her to be. When you try to make her change, in essence, you are telling God He didn't get it right. Let her be her.

The Bible says, "**And the Lord God said, 'It is not good for man to be alone; I will make him a helper comparable to him**.'" Let her help you! That's why God gave her to you. Sadly, most men are too proud to ask God for help, let alone their wife.

I believe the biggest problem is that we 'fixers' view two becoming one as us molding them into us. Nevertheless, it is God molding the two of us into Him. It is like we are round holes and our wives are square pegs. The logical thing for a 'fixer' is to chisel, hammer, and sand the square peg, until it fits into the round hole. After all, there is nothing wrong with the round hole. The square peg has the issues. God is not turning her into a round peg nor is He turning you into a square hole. In reality, only God can take the two and mold into a unique shape that is neither round nor square.

SIDEBAR: Adam had a life before he had a wife. He had a house before he had a spouse.

Your help meet is to help you fulfill your destiny, not fulfill your dreams. She is not to help meet the mortgage. Don't lay a guilt trip on your wife about the bills. She doesn't need to get a job as much as you need to live within your means. If she wants to be a stay-at-home wife, let her. I realize that in today's economy it is difficult for some households to survive on one income. Yet and still, do you really need a $50,000 SUV and 600 channels on your plasma! Make the necessary adjustments. Believe God that if your wife wants to stay at home, He will continue to supply all your need according to His riches in glory in Christ Jesus. I dare you to believe God to be able to tell your wife she can quit her job if she wants to, because you aren't depending on her check to stay afloat. If she wants to continue to work, let her do with her check whatever she pleases. Let her help you fulfill your destiny. Let her be in your corner saying you're the man. Let her be your cheerleader, rooting you on. Come on, brother, be her hero and let her be super!

Sheila is the complete compliment to the fulfillment of my destiny. She doesn't complete me; I'm complete in Him. Nevertheless, she compliments me to the degree that without her, I feel incomplete. In other words, she is like the sugar in my coffee, the peaches in my cobbler, the honey in my tea; she is the complete compliment! All of those things can stand alone, but once the compliments are added, it's difficult to go back to the way it was. She is not my better half; she is my whole. I didn't marry half a woman nor did she marry half a man. We two are one whole in Him, not two halves.

Brothers, listen to me. Some of you are experiencing serious stress, struggle, and strain all because of your S.O.P. a.k.a. Statement of Pride. Most men's Statement of Pride is, "I got this." Usually that leads to them being S.O.S., or Stuck on Stupid. Brothers, refer to the right manual. Get rid of your manly S.O.P. and refer to your Bible. God made her and gave her to you. Let her help you fulfill your destiny. Don't allow your pride to cause you to have a couch ministry for the night. Pride is like a freshly prepared salad. It needs to be eaten, because left to itself; it will eventually stink up the entire house. Swallow your pride men before you stink up your marriage.

What I find to be most comical is the same men who won't let their wives be a helper are the ones who are always trying to make their wives be a help meet. Brothers throughout the body of Christ are frustrated, disillusioned, and hard to get along with, because they can't seem to be able to make their wives get 'it'. What is 'it', anyway? God never told you to make your wife 'it' in the first place. He has already done that. She is not your project. She didn't come in a box that said some assembly required. Take your tool belt off. There are no tool boxes allowed in the throne room. Your wife doesn't need you to assemble her; she needs you to allow her.

Men who aren't busy making their wives are trying to teach them. You can't teach her to be what you never have been nor ever will be! You are not a woman! What are you teaching her? How long does this school last? Is she an average student or on your honor roll? Once you've taught her, then what? If she fails, will she have to repeat being a wife 101? Is she your only pupil, or are you scouting for other potential future students?

All jokes aside, I know there are several things we can teach our wives. However, there are quite a few things she can teach us. Notwithstanding, that's when the real problem begins. A lot of men I know are too proud to let their wife teach them anything. If she makes the suggestion, it is immediately rejected. It's as if she is not allowed to give her input on your marriage. God forbid, she hears a word from the Lord for you. She can hear God for everyone else accept you? Get over your esteem issues and let your wife be your wife.

If you want peace in your home, stop making your wife, stop teaching your wife, stop telling your wife, and start letting your wife.

Chapter 8

LAVISH HER

Proverbs 31:10-31 describes the attributes of a virtuous woman. I personally refer to this portrait of a virtuous wife as the 'Sheila Scriptures'. Every time I read this passage of scripture, I can't help but to thank God for blessing me with such a priceless jewel. What I find so amazing is how God refers to her as being worth far above rubies, yet many husbands don't value their God-given jewel on the same level.

'Sheila Scripture' 28 and 29 says, **"Her children rise up and call her blessed; her husband also, and he praises her: "Many daughters have done well, but you excel them all."**

The word praise is the Hebrew verb meaning to praise, commend, boast, or to shine. To boast is to brag on or be proud of. To shine is to be visible, brilliant; to polish or glow. Now ask yourself, do I publicly boast on my wife or roast on her? Do I ensure that my wife glows or is she so well hidden; no one knows I'm married?

SIDEBAR: Public affirmation leads to private celebration!

It is my job to keep my wife glowing. I purpose in my heart to lavish her. Lavish is defined as abundant, generous; excessive, to spend money on. That's right, to spend money on in excess. In case you were wondering, a gift only on the 'Big 3' (anniversary, birthday and Christmas) is average not excessive. Isn't your queen worth some 'just because' gifts. I love Sheila too much to wait for a holiday to roll around again before I give her a gift.

Some brothers always seem to have an excuse for not lavishing their wives. An excuse is nothing more than the manifestation of an unwilling heart. If I suggest buying her flowers, you say she's allergic. If I say take her shopping, you say she is too indecisive. If I mention taking her to a romantic restaurant, you say you can't find a babysitter. I have the excuse eliminator. Ecclesiastes 10:19 says, "**A feast is made for laughter, and wine makes merry; but money answers everything.**" From now on when you don't know how to lavish her, give her some money and let her determine what she wants.

Some of you may need to meet George Jetson. The 'Jetsons' was a cartoon I used to watch when I was a little boy. It would come on with George giving a few dollars to his daughter Judy and a few more to his son Elroy. On the other hand, Jane, his wife, took the whole wallet. Some wives actually get an allowance from their husband, when they should be allowed to take it all. I want you brothers to practice drawing your wallet like 'Doc' Holiday drew his six-shooter. That's right, practice. When she calls out, 'honey', before she can get her request out of her mouth, draw your wallet. You can't be a stingy husband. My pastor in Saint Louis used to always say romance without finance will become a nuisance. In other words, a booth for two at the burger barn is going to get old.

The truth of the matter is it isn't even in the amount of money you spend on her, as much as it is how you treat her. If all you can afford is a cubic zirconium; buy her the best one you can. Just make sure you always treat her like a priceless jewel.

Sometimes all your wife needs to know is that you are interested in the little things. It's the minute things I do for Sheila that show her how precious she is to me. Something as simple as buying her those little Hershey chocolates with the toffee and caramel, or making sure she has starburst in her office. She likes to crochet, so I go yarn shopping with her. I never knew my contribution in her yarn selection would make her so happy. I'm a smart man. I've become a yarn connoisseur. I make it my business to lavish her in everything I do for her. My goal is to make her feel like the queen I know she is. What is so wrong with opening her door? Instead of waiting for her to wait on you, become her personal valet. Set aside special days and events to celebrate your precious, priceless, God-given jewel. Pour it on. Be excessive. Make her feel like a billion bucks.

Let's look at 'Sheila Scripture' 28 again, **"Her children *rise up* and call her blessed; her husband *also*, and he praises her."** (Italics mine)

Rise up and *also* indicate that this occurred every morning from her children and her husband. You can't be Dr. Jeckle one day and Mr. Hyde the next. She needs consistent praise from you. I have found it's when Sheila is feeling her worst that she needs praise the most. Too many husbands abandon their wives during the most crucial times. For instance, when she is on her menstrual cycle or having PMS, this is not the time to leave her to herself. I decided, when Sheila is menstruating, I will do the PMS-ing. I will Pamper My Sweetheart. What better time to let her know how blessed I am to have her; how I thank God daily for His Son, His Spirit, and my Sheila. I also discovered Purchasing More Stuff helps ease her cramps.

Ephesians 5:28, 29 reads, "**So husbands ought to love their own wives as their own bodies; for no one ever hated his own flesh, but nourishes and cherishes it, just as the Lord does the church.**"

The Greek word for cherish is *thalpo*, which means to keep warm, to foster with tender care. We need look no further than Christ Himself on how to cherish our wives. He holds us as His prized possession. We are forever on His mind. All that He has done, is doing, and will do is concerning His wife, the church.

Serving the Lord is an honor, not a duty, all because of how well He treats me. Never has He spoken a harsh word to me. Never has He given me a cold shoulder. Never has He said, "I told you so." Never has He said, "Not now, I'm busy." Christ cherishes me beyond my greatest expectations. It is an honor and a privilege to be called His wife.

I charge you mighty men of valor to cherish your wives, as Christ does His church. Go out of your way to show her how thankful you are for her. Let her know everyday how much she means to you.

When I think of lavishing my wife, I'm reminded of the Lord's example of servitude. Matthew 20:28 says, "**Just as the Son of Man did not come to be served, but to serve and give His life a ransom for many.**" Jesus said He came to serve! In John 13:5, Jesus washed His disciples' feet. Do you recall the last time you rubbed your wife's feet? Following Christ's example, we should seek out opportunities to serve our queens, lavishly. It is a simple matter of preferring your wife over yourself. Allow your actions and words to become excuse eliminators. Of this I am confident, if you go out of your way to sweep her off her feet; she will go out of her way to keep you off yours! Selah!

~Treat Her Like a Lady!

Come Worship With Us
@
Destiny Christian Center

Praise the Lord! We welcome you to come out and visit one of our awesome worship services.

Service times: Sunday morning at 10:00, Wednesday evening at 7:00

Location: 800 North Bruce Street, Las Vegas, NV 89101

We look forward to seeing you soon!

Pastors Robert & Sheila Poole

Resources

For speaking engagements, other resources, or information about hosting a Making Your Marriage Marvelous conference in your area, please contact us at:

Destiny Christian Center
800 N. Bruce Street
Las Vegas, NV 89101

702-383-0777

Or visit us on the web at www.dcclvonline.com